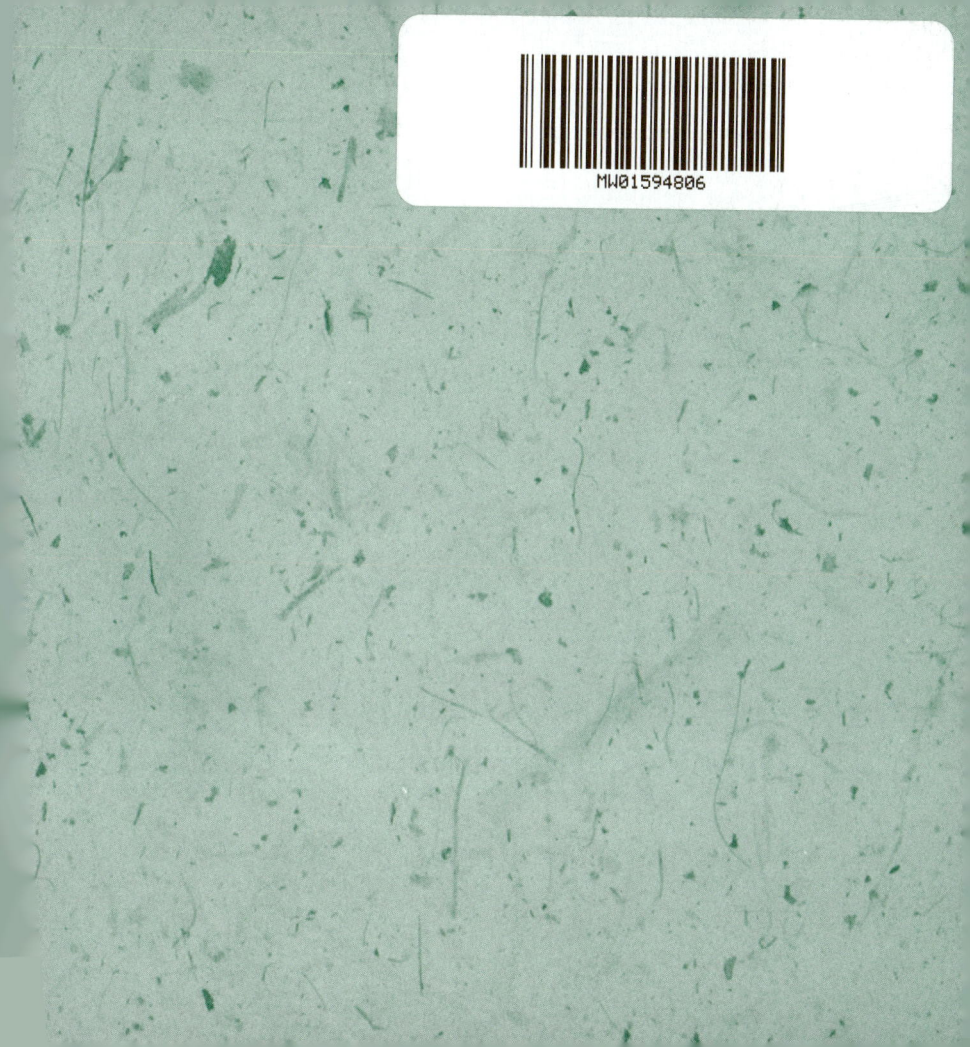

MW01594806

Presented to

_____

By

_____

On

_____

God our Father loved us and by his kindness gave us
everlasting encouragement and good hope.
2 Thessalonians 2:16

The Book of Encouragement

WORLD
PUBLISHING

Grand Rapids, Michigan 49418 U.S.A.

Developed and produced by The Livingstone Corporation. Project staff include: Amber Rae, Carol Smith, and Christopher D. Hudson. Cover and interior design by Design Corps.

ISBN 0529-10862-3

Library of Congress Catalog Card Number 97-062291

Published by: World Publishing, Inc.
                Grand Rapids, Michigan 49418 U.S.A.
                All rights reserved.

Printed in the United States of America

1 2 3 4 5 6 7 8 02 01 00 99 98

RRD-C

Table of Contents

ENCOURAGEMENT FOR THE ONE:

7   Who's wondering if God is listening

13   Who feels inadequate

21   Who's grieving

29   Who's weary

33   Who's afraid

41   Who's lonely

47   Who's anxious

ENCOURAGEMENT TO:

53   Seek God

59   Trust God

67   Have hope

73   Persevere in doing good

ENCOURAGEMENT IN:

79   Want

87   An uncertain future

91   Illness

95   Temptation

111   Stress

115   Hardships, trials & difficulties

Who's wondering if God is listening

God is a God who hears. God listens for the voices of his children. Whether you cry to him in your distress, sing to him in your joy, or simply approach him with a desire to connect, God hears you and will respond.

The LORD is near to everyone who prays to him,
    to every faithful person who prays to him.
He fills the needs of those who fear him.
He hears their cries for help and saves them.

Psalm 145:18-19

We are confident that God listens to us if we ask for anything that has his approval. We know that he listens to our requests. So we know that we already have what we ask him for.

1 John 5:14-15

Know that the LORD singles out godly people
    for himself.
    The LORD hears me when I call to him.

Psalm 4:3

The Lord's eyes are on righteous people.
His ears hear their cry for help.

Psalm 34:15

⌊Righteous people⌋ cry out.
    The Lord hears and rescues them
        from all their troubles.
The Lord is near
    to those whose hearts are humble.
He saves those whose spirits are crushed.

Psalm 34:17-18

If I had thought about doing anything sinful,
   the Lord would not have listened ⌊to me⌋.
But God has heard me.
   He has paid attention to my prayer.
Thanks be to God,
   who has not rejected my prayer
      or taken away his mercy from me.

Psalm 66:18-20

When I was in trouble, I cried out to the LORD,
   and he answered me.

Psalm 120:1

The LORD is far from wicked people,
   but he hears the prayers of righteous people.

Proverbs 15:29

I love the LORD because he hears my voice,
    my pleas for mercy.
I will call on him as long as I live
    because he turns his ear toward me.
The ropes of death became tangled around me.
    The horrors of the grave took hold of me.
        I experienced pain and agony.
But I kept calling on the name of the LORD:
    "Please, LORD, rescue me!"
The LORD is merciful and righteous.
Our God is compassionate.
The LORD protects defenseless people.
    When I was weak, he saved me.
Be at peace again, my soul,
    because the LORD has been good to you.

Psalm 116:1-7

The LORD will never desert his people
   or abandon those who belong to him.

Psalm 94:14

How precious are your thoughts concerning me,
      O God!
How vast in number they are!
   If I try to count them,
      there would be more of them
         than there are grains of sand.
      When I wake up, I am still with you.

Psalm 139:17-18

ENCOURAGEMENT FOR THE ONE

Who feels inadequate

Sometimes it seems like everyone else is going faster, getting better, enjoying life more than we are. Sometimes we feel like we just don't measure up anywhere, anytime. We need to remember that life is not a race, it is a journey. Our final destination is guaranteed, not because of our achievements, but beause we are God's valuable children.

You are people who are holy to the LORD your God.
Out of all the people who live on earth, the LORD has
chosen you to be his own special possession.

Deuteronomy 14:2

Praise the God and Father of our Lord Jesus Christ!
Through Christ, God has blessed us with every spiritual
blessing that heaven has to offer. Before the creation of
the world, he chose us through Christ to be holy and
perfect in his presence. Because of his love he had
already decided to adopt us through Jesus Christ. He
freely chose to do this so that the kindness he had given
us in his dear Son would be praised and given glory.

Ephesians 1:3-6

You alone created my inner being.
You knitted me together inside my mother.
I will give thanks to you

because I have been so amazingly
and miraculously made.
Your works are miraculous,
and my soul is fully aware of this.
My bones were not hidden from you
when I was being made in secret,
when I was being skillfully woven
in an underground workshop.
Your eyes saw me when I was only a fetus.
Every day ⌊of my life⌋ was recorded in your book
before one of them had taken place.
How precious are your thoughts concerning me,
O God!
How vast in number they are!
If I try to count them,
there would be more of them
than there are grains of sand.
When I wake up, I am still with you.

Psalm 139:13-18

Brothers and sisters, consider what you were when God called you to be Christians. Not many of you were wise from a human point of view. You were not in powerful positions or in the upper social classes. But God chose what the world considers nonsense to put wise people to shame. God chose what the world considers weak to put what is strong to shame. God chose what the world considers ordinary and what it despises—what it considers to be nothing—in order to destroy what it considers to be something. As a result, no one can brag in God's presence. You are partners with Christ Jesus because of God. Jesus has become our wisdom sent from God, our righteousness, our holiness, and our ransom from sin. As Scripture says, "Whoever brags must brag about what the Lord has done."

1 Corinthians 1:26-31

By ourselves we are not qualified in any way to claim that we can do anything. Rather, God makes us qualified.

2 Corinthians 3:5

But the LORD told Samuel, "Don't look at his appearance or how tall he is, because I have rejected him. God does not see as humans see. Humans look at outward appearances, but the LORD looks into the heart."

1 Samuel 16:7

The evidence of the Spirit's presence is given to each person for the common good of everyone. The Spirit gives one person the ability to speak with wisdom. The same Spirit gives another person the ability to speak with knowledge. To another person the same Spirit gives ⌊courageous⌋ faith. To another person the same Spirit gives the ability to heal. Another can work

miracles. Another can speak what God has revealed. Another can tell the difference between spirits. Another can speak in different kinds of languages. Another can interpret languages. There is only one Spirit who does all these things by giving what God wants to give to each person.

For example, the body is one unit and yet has many parts. As all the parts form one body, so it is with Christ. By one Spirit we were all baptized into one body. Whether we are Jewish or Greek, slave or free, God gave all of us one Spirit to drink.

As you know, the human body is not made up of only one part, but of many parts. Suppose a foot says, "I'm not a hand, so I'm not part of the body!" Would that mean it's no longer part of the body? Or suppose an ear says, "I'm not an eye, so I'm not a part of the body!" Would that mean it's no longer part of the body? If the whole body were an eye, how could it hear? If the whole

body were an ear, how could it smell? So God put each and every part of the body together as he wanted it. How could it be a body if it only had one part? So there are many parts but one body.

An eye can't say to a hand, "I don't need you!" Or again, the head can't say to the feet, "I don't need you!" The opposite is true. The parts of the body that we think are weaker are the ones we really need. The parts of the body that we think are less honorable are the ones we give special honor. So our unpresentable parts are made more presentable. However, our presentable parts don't need this kind of treatment. God has put the body together and given special honor to the part that doesn't have it. God's purpose was that the body should not be divided but rather that all of its parts should feel the same concern for each other. If one part of the body suffers, all the other parts share its suffering. If one part is praised,

all the others share in its happiness.

You are Christ's body and each of you is an individual part of it.

1 Corinthians 12:7-27

But he told me: "My kindness is all you need. My power is strongest when you are weak." So I will brag even more about my weaknesses in order that Christ's power will live in me. Therefore, I accept weakness, mistreatment, hardship, persecution, and difficulties suffered for Christ. It's clear that when I'm weak, I'm strong.

2 Corinthians 12:9-10

Who's grieving

Grief can cut like a knife and lay our hearts bare and hurting. Grief can rip us open and leave us to struggle through the repairs. But God has a heart of compassion that grieves with us in our sorrows. He holds us together even when we have a broken heart.

Praise the God and Father of our Lord Jesus Christ! He
is the Father who is compassionate and the God who
gives comfort. He comforts us whenever we suffer.
That is why whenever other people suffer, we are able
to comfort them by using the same comfort we have
received from God. Because Christ suffered so much
for us, we can receive so much comfort from him.
Besides, if we suffer, it brings you comfort and salvation. If we are comforted, we can effectively comfort
you when you endure the same sufferings that we
endure. We have confidence in you. We know that as
you share our sufferings, you also share our comfort.

2 Corinthians 1:3-7

Blessed are those who mourn.
They will be comforted.

Matthew 5:4

I heard a loud voice from the throne say, "God lives with humans! God will make his home with them, and they will be his people. God himself will be with them and be their God. He will wipe every tear from their eyes. There won't be any more death. There won't be any grief, crying, or pain, because the first things have disappeared."

Revelation 21:3-4

Brothers and sisters, we don't want you to be ignorant about those who have died. We don't want you to grieve like other people who have no hope. We believe that Jesus died and came back to life. We also believe that, through Jesus, God will bring back those who have died. They will come back with Jesus. We are telling you what the Lord taught. We who are still alive when the Lord comes will not go ⌐into his kingdom⌐ ahead of those who have already died. The

Lord will come from heaven with a command, with the voice of the archangel, and with the trumpet ⌊call⌋ of God. First, the dead who believed in Christ will come back to life. Then, together with them, we who are still alive will be taken in the clouds to meet the Lord in the air. In this way we will always be with the Lord. So then, comfort each other with these words!

1 Thessalonians 4:13-18

You have seen ⌊it⌋; yes, you have taken note
    of trouble and grief
    and placed them under your control.
      The victim entrusts himself to you.
You alone have been the helper of orphans.

Psalm 10:14

Precious in the sight of the LORD
    is the death of his faithful ones.

Psalm 116:15

On this mountain he will remove
   the veil of grief covering all people
     and the mask covering all nations.
He will swallow up death forever.
The Almighty Lord will wipe away tears
   from every face,
   and he will remove the disgrace of his people
     from the whole earth.
   The Lord has spoken.

Isaiah 25:7-8

God loved the world this way: He gave his only Son
so that everyone who believes in him will not die
but will have eternal life.

John 3:16

The God who is in his holy dwelling place
　　is the father of the fatherless
　　　　and the defender of widows.

Psalm 68:5

He has given his people a strong leader,
　　someone praiseworthy for his faithful ones,
　　　　for the people of Israel,
　　　　　　the people who are close to him.
Hallelujah!

Psalm 148:14

He was despised and rejected by people.
He was a man of sorrows, familiar with suffering.
He was despised like one
　　from whom people turn their faces,
　and we didn't consider him to be worth anything.
He certainly has taken upon himself our suffering
　　and carried our sorrows,

but we thought that God had wounded him,
beat him, and punished him.

Isaiah 53:3-4

My sheep respond to my voice, and I know who they
are. They follow me, and I give them eternal life.
They will never be lost, and no one will tear them
away from me.

John 10:27-28

Jesus said to her, "I am the one who brings people
back to life, and I am life itself. Those who believe in
me will live even if they die. Everyone who lives and
believes in me will never die. Do you believe that?"

John 11:25-26

I will give those who are weary all they need.
I will refresh everyone who is filled with sorrow.

Jeremiah 31:25

The LORD is near to those whose hearts are humble.
He saves those whose spirits are crushed.

Psalm 34:18

But as Scripture says:
  "No eye has seen,
    no ear has heard,
      and no mind has imagined
        the things that God has prepared
        for those who love him."

1 Corinthians 2:9

ENCOURAGEMENT FOR THE ONE

Who's weary

God has rest for the tired soul. He has refreshment for the weary heart. He knows the emptiness of exhaustion, both physical and emotional, and he can renew you—heart, body, soul and mind. Just fall into his arms of grace and love.

Don't you know?
　　Haven't you heard?
The eternal God, the Lord,
　　　　the Creator of the ends of the earth,
　　doesn't grow tired or become weary.
　　　　His understanding is beyond reach.
He gives strength to those who grow tired
　　and increases the strength
　　　　　of those who are weak.
Even young people grow tired and become weary,
　　and young men will stumble and fall.
Yet, the strength of those who wait with hope
　　　　in the Lord
　　will be renewed.
　　　　They will soar on wings like eagles.
　　　　　They will run and won't become weary.
　　　　　They will walk and won't grow tired.

Isaiah 40:28-31

Think about Jesus, who endured opposition from
sinners, so that you don't become tired and give up.

Hebrews 12:3

Turn your burdens over to the LORD,
    and he will take care of you.
        He will never let the righteous person stumble.

Psalm 55:22

Come to me, all who are tired from carrying heavy
loads, and I will give you rest. Place my yoke over your
shoulders, and learn from me, because I am gentle and
humble. Then you will find rest for yourselves because
my yoke is easy and my burden is light.

Matthew 11:28-30

I will give those who are weary all they need.
I will refresh everyone who is filled with sorrow.

Jeremiah 31:25

God is our refuge and strength,
    an ever-present help in times of trouble.

Psalm 46:1

Trust him at all times, you people.
Pour out your hearts in his presence.
    God is our refuge.

Psalm 62:8

Who's afraid

Fear is the knowledge that life, at times, asks for more than we have to give. It is the knowledge that our resources alone will sometimes not be enough. It is then that we realize we need more than ourselves. Comfort comes in knowing that our trust is in a God who is more than enough.

Be strong and courageous! Don't tremble or be terrified, because the LORD your God is with you wherever you go.

Joshua 1:9

Look! God is my Savior.
I am confident and unafraid,
   because the LORD is my strength and my song.
   He is my Savior.

Isaiah 12:2

The LORD is my light and my salvation.
   Who is there to fear?
The LORD is my life's fortress.
   Who is there to be afraid of?
Evildoers closed in on me to tear me to pieces.
   My opponents and enemies stumbled and fell.
      Even though an army sets up camp against me,

my heart will not be afraid.
Even though a war breaks out against me,
I will still have confidence ⌊in the LORD⌋.

Psalm 27:1-3

You people of Israel, I will help you,
declares the LORD, your Defender,
the Holy One of Israel.

Isaiah 41:14

I'm leaving you peace. I'm giving you my peace. I
don't give you the kind of peace that the world gives.
So don't be troubled or cowardly.

John 14:27

Even when I am afraid, I still trust you.
I praise the word of God.
I trust God.

I am not afraid.
What can mere flesh ⌊and blood⌋ do to me?

Psalm 56:3-4

God is our refuge and strength,
an ever-present help in times of trouble.
That is why we are not afraid
even when the earth quakes
or the mountains topple
into the depths of the sea.
Water roars and foams,
and mountains shake
at the surging waves.
There is a river
whose streams bring joy to the city of God,
the holy place where the Most High lives.
God is in that city.
It cannot fall.

God will help it at the break of dawn.
Nations are in turmoil, and kingdoms topple.
    The earth melts at the sound of ⌊God's⌋ voice.
The Lᴏʀᴅ of Armies is with us.
The God of Jacob is our stronghold.
Come, see the works of the Lᴏʀᴅ,
    the devastation he has brought to the earth.
        He puts an end to wars all over the earth.
           He breaks an archer's bow.
           He cuts spears in two.
           He burns chariots.
Let go ⌊of your concerns⌋!
    Then you will know that I am God.
        I rule the nations.
        I rule the earth.
The Lᴏʀᴅ of Armies is with us.
The God of Jacob is our stronghold.

Psalm 46:1-11

Whoever lives under the shelter of the Most High
    will remain in the shadow of the Almighty.
I will say to the Lord,
    "⌊You are⌋ my refuge and my fortress,
        my God in whom I trust."
He is the one who will rescue you from
        hunters' traps
    and from deadly plagues.
He will cover you with his feathers,
    and under his wings you will find refuge.
        His truth is your shield and armor.
You do not need to fear
    terrors of the night,
    arrows that fly during the day,
    plagues that roam the dark,
    epidemics that strike at noon.
        They will not come near you,
            even though a thousand may fall dead

beside you
or ten thousand at your right side.
You only have to look with your eyes
to see the punishment of wicked people.
You, O LORD, are my refuge!
You have made the Most High your home.
No harm will come to you.
No sickness will come near your house.
He will put his angels in charge of you
to protect you in all your ways.
They will carry you in their hands
so that you never hit your foot
against a rock.
You will step on lions and cobras.
You will trample young lions and snakes.
Because you love me, I will rescue you.
I will protect you because you know my name.
When you call to me, I will answer you.

I will be with you when you are in trouble.
I will save you and honor you.
I will satisfy you with a long life.
I will show you how I will save you.

Psalm 91:1-16

The Lord's eyes are on those
    who do what he approves.
    His ears hear their prayer.
    The Lord confronts those who do evil.
Who will harm you if you are devoted to doing what
is good? But even if you suffer for doing what God
approves, you are blessed. Don't be afraid of those
who want to harm you. Don't get upset.

1 Peter 3:12-14

God didn't give us a cowardly spirit but a spirit of
power, love, and good judgment.

2 Timothy 1:7

Who's lonely

A person can be lonely in the largest of crowds and the smallest of rooms. A person can be lonely in the deepest of griefs and the brightest of successes. No matter where we feel alone, God can reach that place, touch our lives, and give us the comfort of his companionship.

The Lᴏʀᴅ looks down from heaven.
He sees all of Adam's descendants.
From the place where he sits enthroned,
    he looks down upon all who live on earth.
The one who formed their hearts
    understands everything they do.

Psalm 33:13-15

The Lᴏʀᴅ is near to everyone who prays to him,
    to every faithful person who prays to him.

Psalm 145:18

O Lᴏʀᴅ, you have examined me,
        and you know me.
    You alone know when I sit down
            and when I get up.
    You read my thoughts from far away.
    You watch me when I travel and when I rest.
    You are familiar with all my ways.

Even before there is a ⌊single⌋ word
    on my tongue,
      you know all about it, Lord.
You are all around me—in front of me
    and in back of me.
You lay your hand on me.
    Such knowledge is beyond my grasp.
    It is so high I cannot reach it.
Where can I go ⌊to get away⌋ from your Spirit?
Where can I run ⌊to get away⌋ from you?
    If I go up to heaven, you are there.
    If I make my bed in hell, you are there.
    If I climb upward on the rays of the morning sun
      ⌊or⌋ land on the most distant shore of the sea
        where the sun sets,
      even there your hand would guide me
      and your right hand
        would hold on to me.
If I say, "Let the darkness hide me

and let the light around me turn into night,"
  even the darkness is not too dark
    for you.
  Night is as bright as day.
  Darkness and light are the same ˪to you˩.

Psalm 139:1-12

My eyes are always on the LORD.
  He removes my feet from traps.
Turn to me, and have pity on me.
  I am lonely and oppressed.
Relieve my troubled heart,
  and bring me out of my distress.

Psalm 25:15-17

The LORD answered, "My presence will go ˪with
you,˩ and I will give you peace."

Exodus 33:14

Yet, I am always with you.
　　You hold on to my right hand.
　　　　With your advice you guide me,
　　　　　　and in the end you will take me to glory.
As long as I have you,
　　I don't need anyone else in heaven or on earth.
My body and mind may waste away,
　　but God remains the foundation of my life
　　　　and my inheritance forever.

Psalm 73:23-26

And remember that I am always with you until the
end of time.

Matthew 28:20

The LORD is good.
　　⌊He is⌋ a fortress in the day of trouble.
　　He knows those who seek shelter in him.

Nahum 1:7

The LORD your God is with you.
He is a hero who saves you.
He happily rejoices over you,
renews you with his love,
and celebrates over you
with shouts of joy.

Zephaniah 3:17

ENCOURAGEMENT FOR THE ONE

Who's anxious

Anxiety drains our energy and distracts us from our tasks. It wears us out emotionally. Anxiety robs us of the joy we can have if we would trust God instead. Turning our cares over to God will make more of a difference than our worry ever will.

Turn all your anxiety over to God because he cares
for you.

1 Peter 5:7

So I tell you to stop worrying about what you will
eat, drink, or wear. Isn't life more than food and the
body more than clothes?

Look at the birds. They don't plant, harvest, or
gather the harvest into barns. Yet, your heavenly
Father feeds them. Aren't you worth more than they?

Can any of you add a single hour to your life by
worrying?

And why worry about clothes? Notice how the
flowers grow in the field. They never work or spin
yarn for clothes. But I say that not even Solomon in
all his majesty was dressed like one of these flowers.
That's the way God clothes the grass in the field.
Today it's alive, and tomorrow it's thrown into an

incinerator. So how much more will he clothe you
people who have so little faith?

Don't ever worry and say, "What are we going to
eat?" or "What are we going to drink?" or "What are
we going to wear?" Everyone is concerned about these
things, and your heavenly Father certainly knows you
need all of them. But first, be concerned about his
kingdom and what has his approval. Then all these
things will be provided for you.

So don't ever worry about tomorrow. After all,
tomorrow will worry about itself. Each day has
enough trouble of its own.

Matthew 6:25-34

Let go ⌊of your concerns⌋!
    Then you will know that I am God.
        I rule the nations.
        I rule the earth.

Psalm 46:10

Turn your burdens over to the LORD,
   and he will take care of you.
      He will never let the righteous person stumble.

Psalm 55:22

When I said, "My feet are slipping,"
   your mercy, O LORD, continued to hold me up.
When I worried about many things,
   your assuring words soothed my soul.

Psalm 94:18-19

There is lasting peace for those
      who love your teachings.
   Nothing can make those people stumble.

Psalm 119:165

Wisdom sings her song in the streets.
    In the public squares she raises her voice.
    "Gullible people kill themselves
        because of their turning away.
    Fools destroy themselves
        because of their indifference.
    But whoever listens to me will live
        without worry
        and will be free from the dread
        of disaster."

Proverbs 1:20,32-33

I'm leaving you peace. I'm giving you my peace. I
don't give you the kind of peace that the world gives.
So don't be troubled or cowardly.

John 14:27

Never worry about anything. But in every situation let God know what you need in prayers and requests while giving thanks. Then God's peace, which goes beyond anything we can imagine, will guard your thoughts and emotions through Christ Jesus.

Philippians 4:6-7

ENCOURAGEMENT TO

Seek God

It is not enough to seek God only when it is convenient. It is not enough to notice him only in the miraculous. We must ambitiously tackle the task of knowing God because through the experience of coming to know him, we will find true joy.

Desire God's pure word as newborn babies desire milk. Then you will grow in your salvation. Certainly you have tasted that the Lord is good!

1 Peter 2:2-3

We know that the Son of God has come and has given us understanding so that we know the real God. We are in the one who is real, his Son Jesus Christ. This Jesus Christ is the real God and eternal life.

1 John 5:20

Brothers and sisters, because of the blood of Jesus we can now confidently go into the holy place. Jesus has opened a new and living way for us to go through the curtain. (The curtain is his own body.) We have a superior priest in charge of God's house. We have been sprinkled ⌊with his blood⌋ to free us from a guilty conscience, and our bodies have been

washed with clean water. So we must continue to
come ⌞to him⌟ with a sincere heart and strong faith.

Hebrews 10:19-22

My soul thirsts for God, for the living God.
    When may I come to see God's face?

Psalm 42:2

Taste and see that the Lᴏʀᴅ is good.
    Blessed is the person who takes refuge in him.

Psalm 34:8

⌞Then Jesus said,⌟ "I am the true vine, and my Father
takes care of the vineyard. He removes every one of
my branches that doesn't produce fruit. He also
prunes every branch that does produce fruit to make
it produce more fruit.

    "You are already clean because of what I have told

you. Live in me, and I will live in you. A branch cannot produce any fruit by itself. It has to stay attached to the vine. In the same way, you cannot produce fruit unless you live in me.

"I am the vine. You are the branches. Those who live in me while I live in them will produce a lot of fruit. But you can't produce anything without me. Whoever doesn't live in me is thrown away like a branch and dries up. Branches like this are gathered, thrown into a fire, and burned. If you live in me and what I say lives in you, then ask for anything you want, and it will be yours. You give glory to my Father when you produce a lot of fruit and therefore show that you are my disciples."

John 15:1-8

It's not that I've already reached the goal or have already completed the course. But I run to win that

which Jesus Christ has already won for me. Brothers and sisters, I can't consider myself a winner yet. This is what I do: I don't look back, I lengthen my stride, and I run straight toward the goal to win the prize that God's heavenly call offers in Christ Jesus.

Philippians 3:12-14

You need endurance so that after you have done what God wants you to do, you can receive what he has promised.
>Yet, the one who is coming will come soon.
>>He will not delay.
>The person who has God's approval will live by
>>faith.
>But if he turns back,
>>I will not be pleased with him.

Hebrews 10:36-39

We must continue to hold firmly to our declaration
of faith. The one who made the promise is faithful.

Hebrews 10:23

ENCOURAGEMENT TO

Trust God

In a world that is often disappointing, God keeps his word. He delights in honoring his promises. God expects us to trust him. It is our trust, rather than our deeds, through which he grants us righteousness.

Trust the LORD with all your heart,
    and do not rely on your own understanding.
In all your ways acknowledge him,
    and he will make your paths smooth.

Proverbs 3:5-6

During times of trouble I called on the LORD.
    The LORD answered me ⌞and⌟ set me free
        ⌞from all of them⌟.
The LORD is on my side.
    I am not afraid.
        What can mortals do to me?
The LORD is on my side as my helper.
    I will see ⌞the defeat of⌟ those who hate me.
It is better to depend on the LORD
    than to trust mortals.
It is better to depend on the LORD
    than to trust influential people.

Psalm 118:5-9

The LORD is a stronghold for the oppressed,
   a stronghold in times of trouble.
Those who know your name trust you, O LORD,
   because you have never deserted
      those who seek your help.

Psalm 9:9-10

Trust the LORD, and do good things.
Live in the land, and practice being faithful.
Be happy with the LORD,
   and he will give you the desires of your heart.
Entrust your ways to the LORD.
Trust him, and he will act ⌊on your behalf⌋.
   He will make your righteousness shine
         like a light,
         your just cause like the noonday sun.
Surrender yourself to the LORD,
      and wait patiently for him.

Do not be preoccupied with ⌊an evildoer⌋
    who succeeds in his way
    when he carries out his schemes.

Psalm 37:3-7

If you fear the Lord, trust the Lord.
    He is your helper and your shield.

Psalm 115:11

We know that all things work together for the good
of those who love God—those whom he has called
according to his plan.

Romans 8:28

The Lord is waiting to be kind to you.
He rises to have compassion on you.
    The Lord is a God of justice.
        Blessed are all those who wait for him.

Isaiah 30:18

The LORD is good to those who wait for him,
to anyone who seeks help from him.
It is good to continue to hope and wait silently
for the LORD to save us.

Lamentations 3:25-26

Wait with hope for the LORD.
Be strong, and let your heart be courageous.
Yes, wait with hope for the LORD.

Psalm 27:14

I waited patiently for the LORD.
He turned to me and heard my cry for help.
He pulled me out of a horrible pit,
out of the mud and clay.
He set my feet on a rock
and made my steps secure.
He placed a new song in my mouth,
a song of praise to our God.

Many will see this and worship.
They will trust the Lord.
Blessed is the person
who places his confidence in the Lord
and does not rely on arrogant people
or those who follow lies.
You have done many miraculous things,
O Lord my God.
You have made many wonderful plans for us.
No one compares to you!
I will tell others about your miracles,
which are more than I can count.

Psalm 40:1-5

Wait with hope for the Lord, and follow his path,
and he will honor you by giving you the land.
When wicked people are cut off,
you will see it.

Psalm 37:34

My soul is weak from waiting for you to save me.
   My hope is based on your word.

Psalm 119:81

I wait for the LORD, my soul waits,
   and with hope I wait for his word.
My soul waits for the LORD
   more than those who watch for the morning,
   more than those who watch for the morning.
O Israel, put your hope in the LORD,
   because with the LORD there is mercy
      and with him there is unlimited forgiveness.

Psalm 130:5-7

We wait for the Lord.
   He is our help and our shield.
   In him our hearts find joy.
   In his holy name we trust.
Let your mercy rest on us, O Lord,
   since we wait with hope for you.

Psalm 33:20-22

Have hope

There is hope for your heart no matter what kind of road you're walking down. There is light up ahead, no matter how dark it is now. God is a faithful God who brings the best from the worst. Keep hoping.

The reason I can ⌊still⌋ find hope
    is that I keep this one thing in mind:
the LORD's mercy.
    We were not completely wiped out.
    His compassion is never limited.
        It is new every morning.
        His faithfulness is great.
    My soul can say, "The LORD is my lot ⌊in life⌋.
        That is why I find hope in him."
    The LORD is good to those
        who wait for him,
      to anyone who seeks help from him.
    It is good to continue to hope and wait silently
      for the LORD to save us.

Lamentations 3:21-26

Why are you discouraged, my soul?
Why are you so restless?
Put your hope in God,
because I will still praise him.
He is my savior and my God.

Psalm 43:5

Remember the word ⌊you gave⌋ me.
Through it you gave me hope.
This is my comfort in my misery:
Your promise gave me a new life.

Psalm 119:49-50

You are my hiding place and my shield.
My hope is based on your word.

Psalm 119:114

I wait for the LORD, my soul waits,
    and with hope I wait for his word.
My soul waits for the LORD
    more than those who watch for the morning,
    more than those who watch for the morning.
O Israel, put your hope in the LORD,
    because with the LORD there is mercy
        and with him there is unlimited forgiveness.

Psalm 130:5-7

You are my hope, O Almighty LORD.
You have been my confidence
    ever since I was young.
I depended on you before I was born.
    You took me from my mother's womb.
        My songs of praise constantly speak
        about you.

Psalm 71:5-6

But I will always have hope.
  I will praise you more and more.
My mouth will tell about your righteousness,
    about your salvation all day long.
        Even then, it is more than I can understand.
I will come with the mighty deeds
    of the Almighty LORD.
I will praise your righteousness, yours alone.

Psalm 71:14-16

Brothers and sisters, be patient until the Lord comes again. See how farmers wait for their precious crops to grow. They wait patiently for fall and spring rains. You, too, must be patient. Don't give up hope. The Lord will soon be here.

James 5:7-8

God our Father loved us and by his kindness gave us everlasting encouragement and good hope. Together with our Lord Jesus Christ, may he encourage and strengthen you to do and say everything that is good.

2 Thessalonians 2:16-17

Persevere in doing good

Sometimes life seems backwards. It sometimes seems that the evil in the world is far more effective than the good that we do. Don't lose heart. Persist in the things that you know are good, and trust God to bless your efforts.

We can't allow ourselves to get tired of living the right way. Certainly, each of us will receive ⌊everlasting life⌋ at the proper time, if we don't give up.

Galatians 6:9

Only be strong and very courageous, faithfully doing everything in the teachings that my servant Moses commanded you. Don't turn away from them. Then you will succeed wherever you go.

Joshua 1:7

To love God means that we obey his command-ments. Obeying his commandments isn't difficult because everyone who has been born from God has won the victory over the world. Our faith is what wins the victory over the world.

1 John 5:3-4

Blessed are those whose lives have integrity,
    those who follow the teachings of the Lord.
Blessed are those who obey his written instructions.
    They wholeheartedly search for him.
    They do nothing wrong.
    They follow his directions.
You have commanded
    that your guiding principles be carefully followed.
I pray that my ways may become firmly established
    so that I can obey your laws.
      Then I will never feel ashamed
        when I study all your commandments.
I will give thanks to you
    as I learn your regulations, which are based
      on your righteousness.
I will obey your laws.
    Never abandon me.

Psalm 119:1-8

I find joy in the way
   ⌞shown by⌟ your written instructions
   more than I find joy in all kinds of riches.
I want to reflect on your guiding principles
   and study your ways.
Your laws make me happy.
I never forget your word.

Psalm 119:14-16

God our Father loved us and by his kindness gave us everlasting encouragement and good hope. Together with our Lord Jesus Christ, may he encourage and strengthen you to do and say everything that is good.

2 Thessalonians 2:16-17

After all, God's saving kindness has appeared for the benefit of all people. It trains us to avoid ungodly lives filled with worldly desires so that we can live self-controlled, moral, and godly lives in this present world. At the same time we can expect what we hope for—the appearance of the glory of our great God and Savior, Jesus Christ. He gave himself for us to set us free from every sin and to cleanse us so that we can be his special people who are enthusiastic about doing good things.

Titus 2:11-14

We can go to God with bold confidence through faith in Christ.

Ephesians 3:12

When I called, you answered me.
    You made me bold by strengthening my soul.

Psalm 138:3

ENCOURAGEMENT IN

Want

Ultimately God gives us everything we need-

but not always immediately. There are times in

our lives when we struggle, when we want,

when we need. But God does not leave us there.

He will always take care of us wherever we are.

God is my helper!
The Lord is the provider for my life.

Psalm 54:4

He provides food for those who fear him.
He always remembers his promise.

Psalm 111:5

Tell those who have the riches of this world not to
be arrogant and not to place their confidence in
anything as uncertain as riches. Instead, they should
place their confidence in God who richly provides us
with everything to enjoy.

1 Timothy 6:17

Certainly, God is so great
    that he is beyond our understanding.
        The number of his years cannot be counted.
He collects drops of water.
He distills rain from his mist,
    which then drips from the clouds.
    It pours down on many people.
        Can anyone really understand
            how clouds spread out
        or how he thunders
            from his dwelling place?
    Look, he scatters his flashes
        of lightning around him
        and covers the depths of the sea.
This is how he uses the rains to provide for people
    and to give them more than enough food.

Job 36:26-31

You take care of the earth, and you water it.
You make it much richer than it was.
    (The river of God is filled with water.)
You provide grain for them.
    Indeed, you even prepare the ground.
You drench plowed fields ⌊with rain⌋
    and level their clumps of soil.
You soften them with showers
    and bless what grows in them.

Psalm 65:9-10

Fear the LORD, you holy people who belong to him.
    Those who fear him are never in need.
Young lions go hungry and may starve,
    but those who seek the LORD's help
        have all the good things they need.

Psalm 34:9,10

As long as I have you,
  I don't need anyone else in heaven or on earth.
My body and mind may waste away,
  but God remains the foundation of my life
    and my inheritance forever.

Psalm 73:25,26

A thief comes to steal, kill, and destroy. But I came so that my sheep will have life and so that they will have everything they need.

John 10:10

Pay attention to my cry for help, my king
　　and my God,
because I pray only to you.
　　In the morning, O LORD, hear my voice.
　　In the morning I lay my needs
　　　　in front of you,
　　　　and I wait.

Psalm 5:2-3

He raises the poor from the dust.
He lifts the needy from the trash heap
　　in order to make them sit with nobles
　　　　and even to make them inherit a glorious
　　　　throne.
The pillars of the earth are the LORD's.
　　He has set the world on them.

1 Samuel 2:8

You have been a refuge for the poor,
  a refuge for the needy in their distress,
  a shelter from the rain, and shade from the heat.

Isaiah 25:4

Needy people will not always be forgotten.
  Nor will the hope of oppressed people
    be lost forever.

Psalm 9:18

I know that the LORD will defend the rights
  of those who are oppressed
  and the cause of those who are needy.

Psalm 140:12

Don't you know?
Haven't you heard?
The eternal God, the LORD, the Creator
of the ends of the earth,
doesn't grow tired or become weary.
His understanding is beyond reach.
He gives strength to those who grow tired
and increases the strength of those
who are weak.
Even young people grow tired and become weary,
and young men will stumble and fall.
Yet, the strength of those who wait with hope
in the LORD
will be renewed.
They will soar on wings like eagles.
They will run and won't become weary.
They will walk and won't grow tired.

Isaiah 40:28-31

ENCOURAGEMENT IN

An uncertain future

There are many things worse than an uncertain future but few things that feel as uncomfortable. When we face uncertainty, we feel a loss of control over our own lives. We can comfort ourselves knowing that whatever comes we will face it with a powerful God on our side and the grace of his love.

I trust you, O Lord.
I said, "You are my God."
My future is in your hands.
   Rescue me from my enemies,
      from those who persecute me.

Psalm 31:14-15

Do not envy sinners in your heart.
   Instead, continue to fear the Lord.
      There is indeed a future,
         and your hope will never be cut off.

Proverbs 23:17-18

I believe that I will see the goodness of the Lord
   in this world of the living.
Wait with hope for the Lord.
Be strong, and let your heart be courageous.
Yes, wait with hope for the Lord.

Psalm 27:13-14

The LORD is waiting to be kind to you.
He rises to have compassion on you.
　　The LORD is a God of justice.
　　　　Blessed are all those who wait for him.

Isaiah 30:18

I know the plans that I have for you, declares the LORD. They are plans for peace and not disaster, plans to give you a future filled with hope. Then you will call to me. You will come and pray to me, and I will hear you.

Jeremiah 29:11-12

I am convinced that nothing can ever separate us from God's love which Christ Jesus our Lord shows us. We can't be separated by death or life, by angels or rulers, by anything in the present or anything in the future, by forces or powers in the world above or in the world below, or by anything else in creation.

Romans 8:38-39

Tell those who have the riches of this world not to be arrogant and not to place their confidence in anything as uncertain as riches. Instead, they should place their confidence in God who richly provides us with everything to enjoy. Tell them to do good, to do a lot of good things, to be generous, and to share. By doing this they store up a treasure for themselves which is a good foundation for the future. In this way they take hold of what life really is.

1 Timothy 6:17-19

A sinner may commit a hundred crimes and yet live a long life. Still, I know with certainty that it will go well for those who fear God, because they fear him.

Ecclesiastes 8:12

ENCOURAGEMENT IN

Illness

When we are not physically well, our whole outlook is affected. We need God's power to enable us to endure. We need God's healing to enable us to be well again. We need God's presence to guide us through.

O Lord my God,
  I cried out to you for help,
    and you healed me.
O Lord, you brought me up from the grave.
  You called me back to life
    from among those who had gone into the pit.

Psalm 30:2-3

The Lord will support him on his sickbed.
  You will restore this person to health
    when he is ill.

Psalm 41:3

Praise the Lord, my soul!
Praise his holy name, all that is within me.
Praise the Lord, my soul,
  and never forget all the good he has done:
    He is the one who forgives all your sins,

the one who heals all your diseases,
the one who rescues your life from the pit,
the one who crowns you
    with mercy and compassion,
the one who fills your life with blessings
    so that you become young again
        like an eagle.

Psalm 103:1-5

Heal me, O Lord, and I will be healed.
    Rescue me, and I will be rescued.
        You are the one I praise.

Jeremiah 17:14

May my prayer come to you at an acceptable time,
O Lord.
O God, out of the greatness of your mercy,
answer me with the truth of your salvation.
Rescue me from the mud.
Do not let me sink ⌊into it⌋.
I want to be rescued from those who hate me
and from the deep water.
Do not let floodwaters sweep me away.
Do not let the ocean swallow me up,
or the pit close its mouth over me.
Answer me, O Lord, because your mercy is good.
Out of your unlimited compassion, turn to me.
I am in trouble, so do not hide your face from me.
Answer me quickly!
Come close, and defend my soul.
Set me free because of my enemies.

Psalm 69:13-18

Temptation

We sometimes want things that are bad for us.

When we are tempted, we sometimes feel that

we cannot resist. Only through God's power

can we say "No" to our temptations and "Yes"

to God's best for our lives.

There isn't any temptation that you have experienced which is unusual for humans. God, who faithfully keeps his promises, will not allow you to be tempted beyond your power to resist. But when you are tempted, he will also give you the ability to endure the temptation as your way of escape.

1 Corinthians 10:13

Blessed are those who endure when they are tested. When they pass the test, they will receive the crown of life that God has promised to those who love him. When someone is tempted, he shouldn't say that God is tempting him. God can't be tempted by evil, and God doesn't tempt anyone. Everyone is tempted by his own desires as they lure him away and trap him. Then desire becomes pregnant and gives birth to sin. When sin grows up, it gives birth to death.

James 1:12-15

God is faithful and reliable. If we confess our sins, he forgives them and cleanses us from everything we've done wrong.

1 John 1:9

Since we are surrounded by so many examples ⌊of faith⌋, we must get rid of everything that slows us down, especially sin that distracts us. We must run the race that lies ahead of us and never give up. We must focus on Jesus, the source and goal of our faith. He saw the joy ahead of him, so he endured death on the cross and ignored the disgrace it brought him. Then he received the highest position in heaven, the one next to the throne of God. Think about Jesus, who endured opposition from sinners, so that you don't become tired and give up.

Hebrews 12:1-3

May the God who gives peace make you holy in
every way. May he keep your whole being—spirit,
soul, and body—blameless when our Lord Jesus
Christ comes. The one who calls you is faithful, and
he will do this.

1 Thessalonians 5:23-24

What should we say then? Should we continue to
sin so that God's kindness will increase? That's
unthinkable! As far as sin is concerned, we have
died. So how can we still live under sin's influence?

Romans 6:1-2

We know that Christ, who was brought back to life,
will never die again. Death no longer has any power
over him. When he died, he died once and for all to
sin's power. But now he lives, and he lives for God.

So consider yourselves dead to sin's power but living for God in the power Christ Jesus gives you.

Romans 6:9-11

The teachings of the L ORD are perfect.
    They renew the soul.
The testimony of the L ORD is dependable.
    It makes gullible people wise.
The instructions of the L ORD are correct.
    They make the heart rejoice.
The command of the L ORD is radiant.
    It makes the eyes shine.
The fear of the L ORD is pure.
    It endures forever.
The decisions of the L ORD are true.
    They are completely fair.
    They are more desirable than gold,

even the finest gold.
They are sweeter than honey,
even the drippings from a honeycomb.
As your servant I am warned by them.
There is a great reward in following them.
Who can notice every mistake?
Forgive my hidden faults.
Keep me from sinning.
Do not let anyone gain control over me.
Then I will be blameless,
and I will be free from any great offense.
May the words from my mouth
and the thoughts from my heart
be acceptable to you,
O LORD, my rock and my defender.

Psalm 19:7-14

Through the blood of his Son, we are set free from our sins. God forgives our failures because of his overflowing kindness.

Ephesians 1:7

God's divine power has given us everything we need for life and for godliness. This power was given to us through knowledge of the one who called us by his own glory and integrity. Through his glory and integrity he has given us his promises that are of the highest value. Through these promises you will share in the divine nature because you have escaped the corruption that sinful desires cause in the world.

2 Peter 1:3-4

Blessed is the person
    whose disobedience is forgiven
  and whose sin is pardoned.
Blessed is the person whom the Lord
    no longer accuses of sin
  and who has no deceitful thoughts.
When I kept silent ⌊about my sins⌋,
  my bones began to weaken
      because of my groaning all day long.
Day and night your hand lay heavily on me.
My strength shriveled in the summer heat.
I made my sins known to you,
    and I did not cover up my guilt.
I decided to confess them to you, O Lord.
  Then you forgave all my sins.
For this reason let all godly people pray to you
  when you may be found.
      Then raging floodwater will not reach them.

You are my hiding place.
You protect me from trouble.
You surround me with joyous songs of salvation.
⌊The LORD says,⌋
    "I will instruct you.
    I will teach you the way that you should go.
    I will advise you as my eyes watch over you.
Don't be stubborn like a horse or mule.
    ⌊They need⌋ a bit and bridle in their mouth
        to restrain them,
        or they will not come near you."
Many heartaches await wicked people,
    but mercy surrounds those who trust the LORD.
Be glad and find joy in the LORD,
        you righteous people.
Sing with joy, all whose motives are decent.

Psalm 32:1-11

Have pity on me, O God,
    in keeping with your mercy.
  In keeping with your unlimited compassion,
      wipe out my rebellious acts.
Wash me thoroughly from my guilt,
    and cleanse me from my sin.
      I admit that I am rebellious.
      My sin is always in front of me.
I have sinned against you, especially you.
I have done what you consider evil.
  So you hand down justice when you speak,
    and you are blameless when you judge.
Indeed, I was born guilty.
  I was a sinner when my mother conceived me.
Yet, you desire truth and sincerity.
  Deep down inside me you teach me wisdom.
Purify me from sin with hyssop,
    and I will be clean.

Wash me, and I will be whiter than snow.
    Let me hear ⌊sounds of⌋ joy and gladness.
    Let the bones that you have broken dance.
Hide your face from my sins,
    and wipe out all that I have done wrong.
Create a clean heart in me, O God,
    and renew a faithful spirit within me.
Do not force me away from your presence,
    and do not take your Holy Spirit from me.
Restore the joy of your salvation to me,
    and provide me with a spirit
        of willing obedience.

Psalm 51:1-12

O LORD, out of the depths I call to you.
O Lord, hear my voice.
Let your ears be open to my pleas for mercy.
O LORD, who would be able to stand
   if you kept a record of sins?
But with you there is forgiveness
   so that you can be feared.
I wait for the LORD, my soul waits,
   and with hope I wait for his word.
My soul waits for the LORD
   more than those who watch for the morning,
   more than those who watch for the morning.
O Israel, put your hope in the LORD,
   because with the LORD there is mercy
     and with him there is unlimited forgiveness.
     He will rescue Israel from all its sins.

Psalm 130:1-8

Finally, receive your power from the Lord and from his mighty strength. Put on all the armor that God supplies. In this way you can take a stand against the devil's strategies. This is not a wrestling match against a human opponent. We are wrestling with rulers, authorities, the powers who govern this world of darkness, and spiritual forces that control evil in the heavenly world. For this reason, take up all the armor that God supplies. Then you will be able to take a stand during these evil days. Once you have overcome all obstacles, you will be able to stand your ground.

So then, take your stand! Fasten truth around your waist like a belt. Put on God's approval as your breastplate. Put on your shoes so that you are ready to spread the Good News that gives peace. In addition to all these, take the Christian faith as your shield. With it you can put out all the flaming

arrows of the evil one. Also take salvation as your helmet and the word of God as the sword that the Spirit supplies.

Pray in the Spirit in every situation. Use every kind of prayer and request there is. For the same reason be alert. Use every kind of effort and make every kind of request for all of God's people.

Ephesians 6:10-18

The LORD is compassionate, merciful, patient,
    and always ready to forgive.
He will not always accuse us of wrong
    or be angry ⌊with us⌋ forever.
He has not treated us as we deserve for our sins
    or paid us back for our wrongs.
As high as the heavens are above the earth—
    that is how vast his mercy is toward those
        who fear him.

As far as the east is from the west—
    that is how far he has removed
        our rebellious acts from himself.
As a father has compassion for his children,
    so the LORD has compassion
        for those who fear him.

Psalm 103:8-13

Therefore, never let sin rule your physical body so that you obey its desires. Never offer any part of your body to sin's power. No part of your body should ever be used to do any ungodly thing. Instead, offer yourselves to God as people who have come back from death and are now alive. Offer all the parts of your body to God. Use them to do everything that God approves of.

Romans 6:12-13

God can guard you so that you don't fall and so that you can be full of joy as you stand in his glorious presence without fault.

Jude 24

We need to hold on to our declaration of faith: We have a superior chief priest who has gone through the heavens. That person is Jesus, the Son of God. We have a chief priest who is able to sympathize with our weaknesses. He was tempted in every way that we are, but he didn't sin. So we can go confidently to the throne of God's kindness to receive mercy and find kindness, which will help us at the right time.

Hebrews 4:14-16

ENCOURAGEMENT IN

Stress

Our world runs on stress points. Our industries thrive on pressure and productivity. In spite of the busyness of this world we can maintain the serenity that comes from knowing that God is ultimately in control of every calendar and every agenda item.

The LORD supports everyone who falls.
He straightens ⌊the backs⌋ of those
 who are bent over.

Psalm 145:14

Thanks be to the Lord,
 who daily carries our burdens for us.
  God is our salvation.

Psalm 68:19

O Lord, you have been our refuge
  throughout every generation.
 Before the mountains were born,
 before you gave birth to the earth and the world,
  you were God.
  You are God from everlasting to everlasting.

Psalm 90:1-2

Although they scheme and plan evil against you,
  they will not succeed.

Psalm 21:11

The Lord has become my stronghold.
My God has become my rock of refuge.

Psalm 94:22

I call out to you, O Lord.
I say, "You are my refuge,
  my own inheritance in this world of the living."
Pay attention to my cry for help
  because I am very weak.
Rescue me from those who pursue me
  because they are too strong for me.
Release my soul from prison
  so that I may give thanks to your name.
    Righteous people will surround me
      because you are good to me.

Psalm 142:5-7

I look up toward the mountains.
　　Where can I find help?
My help comes from the LORD,
　　the maker of heaven and earth.
He will not let you fall.
　　Your guardian will not fall asleep.
Indeed, the Guardian of Israel
　　never rests or sleeps.
The LORD is your guardian.
The LORD is the shade over your right hand.
　　The sun will not beat down on you
　　　　during the day,
　　nor will the moon at night.
The LORD guards you from every evil.
　　He guards your life.
The LORD guards you as you come and go,
　　now and forever.

Psalm 121:1-8

ENCOURAGEMENT IN

Hardships, trials & difficulties

Sometimes life is counted not day by day, but blow by blow. Sometimes, it's just a hard life. At those times we need a good word, a light thought, a promise that difficulties don't last. Where better to find that word than from God, who knows the worst and best of days and loves us through all of them.

Even if the fig tree does not bloom
    and the vines have no grapes,
even if the olive tree fails to produce
    and the fields yield no food,
even if the sheep pen is empty
    and the stalls have no cattle—
even then,
    I will be happy with the LORD.
    I will truly find joy in God, who saves me.
The LORD Almighty is my strength.
    He makes my feet like those of a deer.
      He makes me walk on the mountains.

Habakkuk 3:17-19

My brothers and sisters, be very happy when you
are tested in different ways. You know that such
testing of your faith produces endurance. Endure
until your testing is over. Then you will be mature
and complete, and you won't need anything.

James 1:2-4

Blessed are those who endure when they are tested.
When they pass the test, they will receive the crown
of life that God has promised to those who love him.

James 1:12

What will separate us from the love Christ has for
us? Can trouble, distress, persecution, hunger,
nakedness, danger, or violent death separate us from
his love? As Scripture says:
   "We are being killed all day long because of you.
   We are thought of as sheep to be slaughtered."

The one who loves us gives us an overwhelming victory in all these difficulties. I am convinced that nothing can ever separate us from God's love which Christ Jesus our Lord shows us. We can't be separated by death or life, by angels or rulers, by anything in the present or anything in the future, by forces or powers in the world above or in the world below, or by anything else in creation.

Romans 8:35-39

The LORD is my shepherd.
    I am never in need.
        He makes me lie down in green pastures.
        He leads me beside peaceful waters.
        He renews my soul.
        He guides me along the paths of righteousness
            for the sake of his name.
    Even though I walk through the dark valley

of death,
because you are with me, I fear no harm.
Your rod and your staff give me courage.
You prepare a banquet for me
while my enemies watch.
You anoint my head with oil.
My cup overflows.
Certainly, goodness and mercy will stay close to me
all the days of my life,
and I will remain in the LORD's house
for days without end.

Psalm 23:1-6

I love you, O LORD, my strength.
The LORD is my rock and my fortress
and my Savior,
my God, my rock in whom I take refuge,
my shield, and the strength of my salvation,

my stronghold.
The LORD should be praised.
I called on him,
and I was saved from my enemies.
The ropes of death had become tangled
around me.
The torrents of destruction
had overwhelmed me.
The ropes of the grave had surrounded me.
The clutches of death had confronted me.
I called on the LORD in my distress.
I cried to my God for help.
He heard my voice from his temple,
and my cry for help reached his ears.

Psalm 18:1-6

We know that all things work together for the good
of those who love God—those whom he has called
according to his plan.

Romans 8:28

The Lord will answer you in times of trouble.
The name of the God of Jacob will protect you.
He will send you help from his holy place
    and support you from Zion.

Psalm 20:1-2

During times of trouble I called on the Lord.
    The Lord answered me ⌊and⌋ set me free
      ⌊from all of them⌋.
The Lord is on my side.
    I am not afraid.
      What can mortals do to me?
The Lord is on my side as my helper.

I will see ⌊the defeat of⌋ those who hate me.
It is better to depend on the LORD
    than to trust mortals.
It is better to depend on the LORD
    than to trust influential people.

Psalm 118:5-9

Trouble and hardship have found me,
    but your commandments ⌊still⌋ make me happy.

Psalm 119:143

That is why we are not discouraged. Though outwardly we are wearing out, inwardly we are renewed day by day. Our suffering is light and temporary and is producing for us an eternal glory that is greater than anything we can imagine.

2 Corinthians 4:16-17

I've told you this so that my peace will be with you.
In the world you'll have trouble. But cheer up! I
have overcome the world.

John 16:33

The Lᴏᴇᴅ is good.
⌞He is⌡ a fortress in the day of trouble.
He knows those who seek shelter in him.

Nahum 1:7

Praise the God and Father of our Lord Jesus Christ! He
is the Father who is compassionate and the God who
gives comfort. He comforts us whenever we suffer.
That is why whenever other people suffer, we are able
to comfort them by using the same comfort we have
received from God. Because Christ suffered so much
for us, we can receive so much comfort from him.
Besides, if we suffer, it brings you comfort and salva-

tion. If we are comforted, we can effectively comfort you when you endure the same sufferings that we endure. We have confidence in you. We know that as you share our sufferings, you also share our comfort.

2 Corinthians 1:3-7

But he told me: "My kindness is all you need. My power is strongest when you are weak." So I will brag even more about my weaknesses in order that Christ's power will live in me. Therefore, I accept weakness, mistreatment, hardship, persecution, and difficulties suffered for Christ. It's clear that when I'm weak, I'm strong.

2 Corinthians 12:9-10

You are my hiding place.
You protect me from trouble.
You surround me with joyous songs of salvation.

Psalm 32:7

The righteous person has many troubles,
    but the LORD rescues him from all of them.

Psalm 34:19

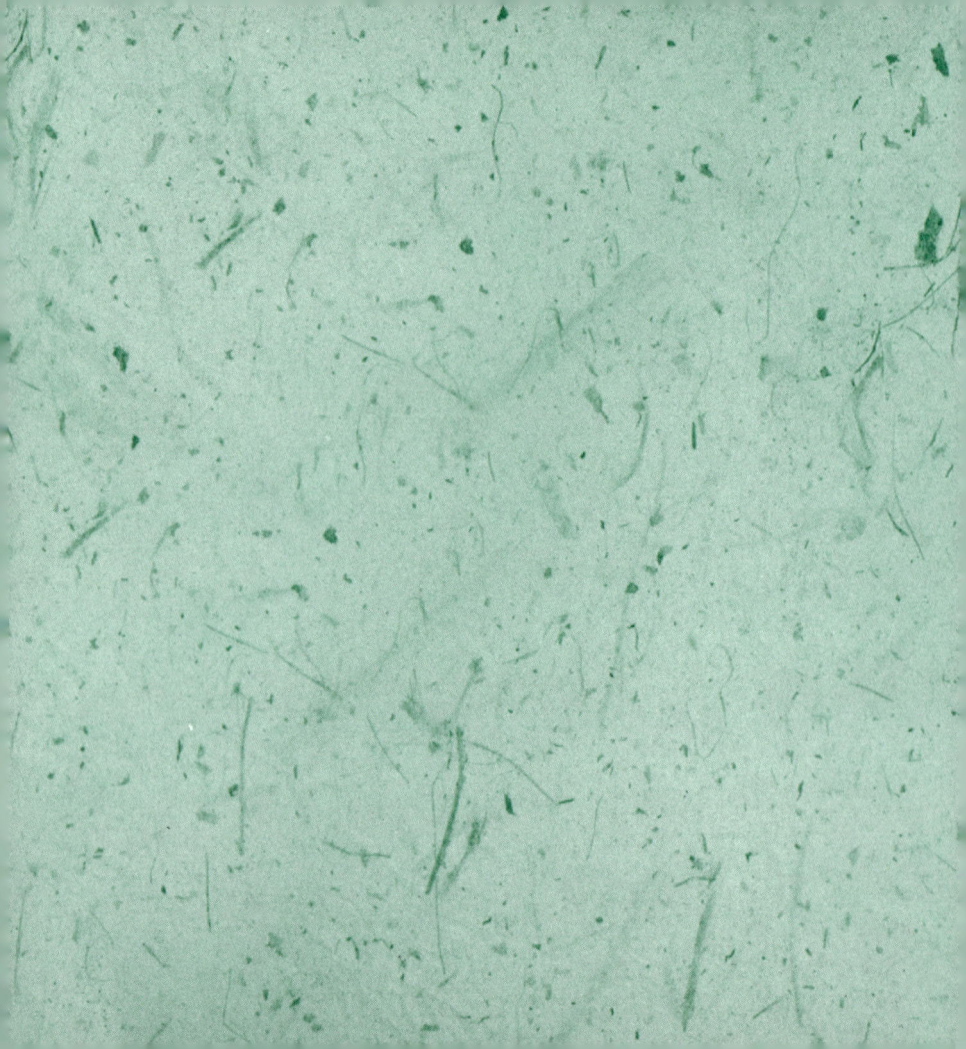